This book belongs to

__AIDEN + BRADLEY__
6/2020
FROM GRAMMY + GRANDPAW

NEIL

This book is dedicated to my children - Mikey, Kobe, and Jojo.
One person can make a differnce.

Earth Ninja

By Mary Nhin

Pictures by
Jelena Stupar

Lazy Ninja threw away his trash. He saw the recyclables bin but didn't fully understand what it was for.

That afternoon, Lazy Ninja and Earth Ninja went to the beach and played in the waves.

Then, suddenly, they noticed a turtle that was lying on the shore, wiggling.

The ninjas walked up to the little guy and noticed he was wrapped in plastic.

"Let's try to remove the plastic," said Earth Ninja.

After a while, Earth Ninja freed the turtle from his plastic chains.

"Wow, how'd he end up like that?" asked Lazy Ninja.

"When we don't throw away our trash properly, a lot of it ends up in the ocean," replied Earth Ninja.

"How?" asked Lazy Ninja.

"We can practice the 3 Rs. Come on. I'll show you," replied Earth Ninja.

Reuse

We can turn used paper into art supplies or scrap paper for notes.

We can use reusable lunch containers instead of plastic wrap or disposable baggies.

And, we can reuse plastic and paper bags as liners for trash cans.

Recycle

We can take the time to recycle glass, paper boxes, and plastic.

Reduce

Riding our bikes or walking can reduce our carbon footprint.

Using uneaten food as fertilizer can reduce food waste.

And making sure we put reusable bags in the car for shopping can reduce plastic waste.

"Yep, we all do," replied Earth Ninja.

Facts

If you lined up the plastic bottles tossed away each year, they would circle our planet FOUR TIMES.

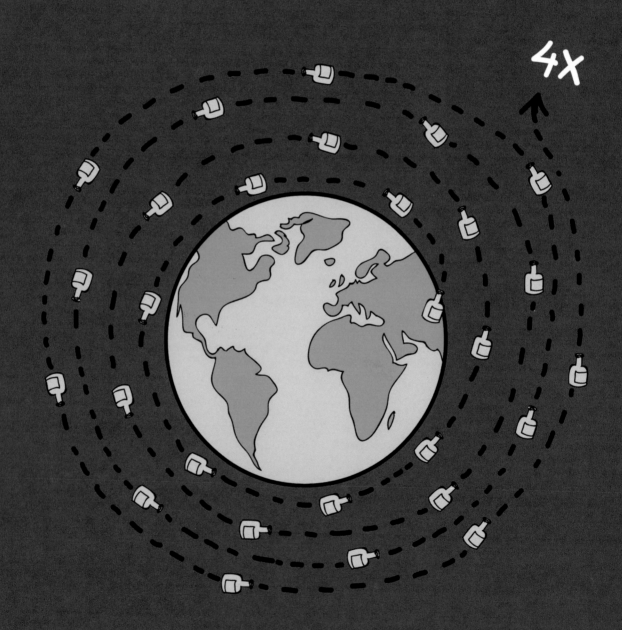

Energy saved from recycling a glass bottle can light a light bulb for FOUR HOURS.

More Facts

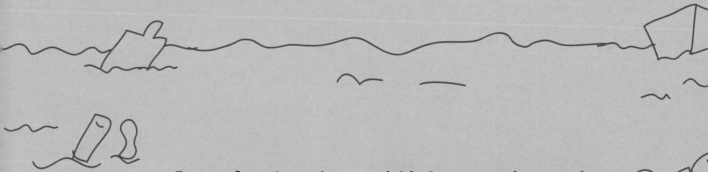

- 75% of garbage is recyclable but we only recycle 30% in the US.

- Plastics discarded into the environment perpetually leach toxic chemicals into the land and sea.

- Our garbage can maim, strangle, and kill marine animals.

- A single soda can sits in a landfill for at least 500 YEARS. All aluminium cans may be recycled.

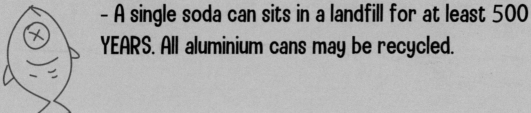

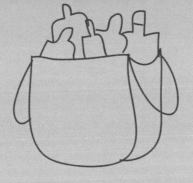

What you can do

- Reduce

- Reuse

- Recycle

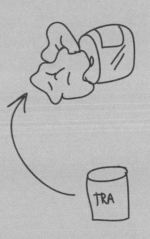

Every single action to combat ninja waste counts!

Sign up for new Ninja book releases at GrowGrit.co

Made in the USA
Monee, IL
05 May 2020